DISCOVER

French Explorers

by Barbara Brannon

Table of Contents

Introduction

Many people **explored North America**.
Many people explored for **France**.

▲ **France explored North America.**

Asia

explored

explorer

France

North America

river

What Did Jacques Cartier Do?

Cartier explored North America. Cartier explored for France.

▲ **Cartier was an explorer.**

Cartier explored North America. Cartier explored a great **river**.

▲ Cartier explored the Saint Lawrence River.

It's a Fact

Jacques Cartier met native people.

Cartier explored to find **Asia**.

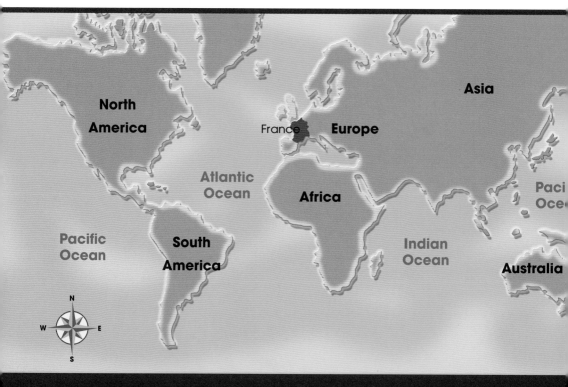

North
America

France **Europe**

Asia

Atlantic
Ocean

Africa

Paci
Oce

Pacific
Ocean

South
America

Indian
Ocean

Australia

N
W   E
S

▲ **Cartier tried to go to Asia.**

Cartier explored lands by the river.

Did You Know?

Cartier explored to find the Northwest Passage.

What Did Samuel de Champlain Do?

Champlain explored North America. Champlain explored for France.

Champlain explored North America. Champlain explored a great river.

▲ Champlain explored the Saint Lawrence River.

Champlain explored to find land.

▲ Champlain explored North America.

Champlain explored to make maps.

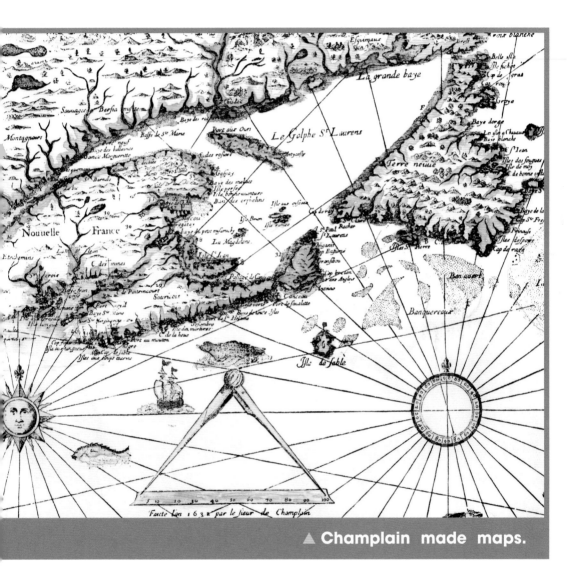

▲ **Champlain made maps.**

What Did Sieur de La Salle Do?

La Salle explored North America. La Salle explored for France.

▲ La Salle was an explorer.

▲ La Salle explored in a canoe.

La Salle explored North America.

La Salle explored the Great Lakes.

▲ La Salle explored four lakes.

▲ **La Salle explored with native people.**

La Salle explored the Mississippi River. La Salle explored the Mississippi River Valley.

Did You Know?

La Salle also had a ship. The ship sank. People found the ship in 1995.

Conclusion

Many people explored for France.

▲ Cartier explored for France.

▲ Champlain explored for France.

▲ La Salle explored for France.

Concept Map

French Explorers

What Did Jacques Cartier Do?

- explored North America
- explored to find Asia
- explored a great river

What Did Samuel de Champlain Do?

- explored North America
- explored a great river
- explored to find land
- explored to make maps

What Did Sieur de La Salle Do?

- explored North America
- explored the Great Lakes
- explored the Mississippi River
- explored the Mississippi River Valley

Glossary

Asia a large continent

*Cartier explored to find **Asia**.*

explored went to new places

*La Salle **explored** North America.*

explorer a person who goes to new places

*Cartier was an **explorer**.*

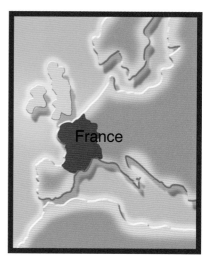

France a country in Europe

*Champlain explored for **France**.*

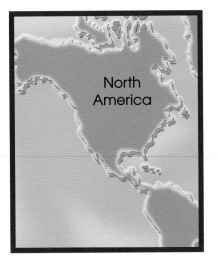

North America a continent

La Salle explored
North America.

river a long, moving body
of water

*Cartier explored a
great **river***.

Index